THE ADVENTURES OF ODYSSEUS

MYTHOLOGY STORIES FOR KIDS

CHILDREN'S FOLK TALES & MYTHS

BABY PROFESSOR

EDUCATION KIDS

Speedy Publishing LLC

40 E. Main St. #1156

Newark, DE 19711

www.speedypublishing.com

Copyright 2017

Odysseus was one of the greatest adventurers in Greek mythology. But what did he actually do? Let's find out!

KING OF ITHACA

Odysseus (called Ulysses by the Romans) was the king of Ithaca, a kingdom on an island in Greece. His father, who had been king, had retired to a quiet life.

ANCIENT STATUE OF ODYSSEUS

ITHACA ISLAND IN GREECE

Odysseus was one of the great heroes of Greece. He was a strong leader, a bold fighter, and a fast thinker. He could come up with a tall story quickly, and sometimes could beat his opponent with words, without ever having to draw his weapon.

Odysseus was married to Penelope, and their son was Telemachus. He had a happy marriage, but outside events called him away.

EUCHARIS AND TELEMACHUS

ANCIENT CITY OF TROY

Helen was the most beautiful woman in the Greek world, and many men wanted to marry her. She married Menelaus, another Greek king; but soon after Paris, a prince of Troy, won Helen's heart and stole her away.

Menelaus called on all the kings of Greece to support him in getting his wife back. This would involve fighting a war with Troy, which was a powerful city.

THE ROMAN SCULPTURE OF MENELAUS

STATUE OF ODYSSEUS

Odysseus did not want to go off on a war to solve someone else's marriage problems. He pretended to have lost his mind, but Menelaus' messengers saw through the trick. Now Odysseus had no choice but to gather his men and lead them to war as part of the Greek army.

Odysseus may not have wanted to go to war, but once he was on his way he was a leader of the Greek effort. The Greek fleet landed near Troy and made camp along the shore. For the next nine years the Greek army tried to travel the last few hundred yards and conquer the city.

THE GREEKS AT TROY

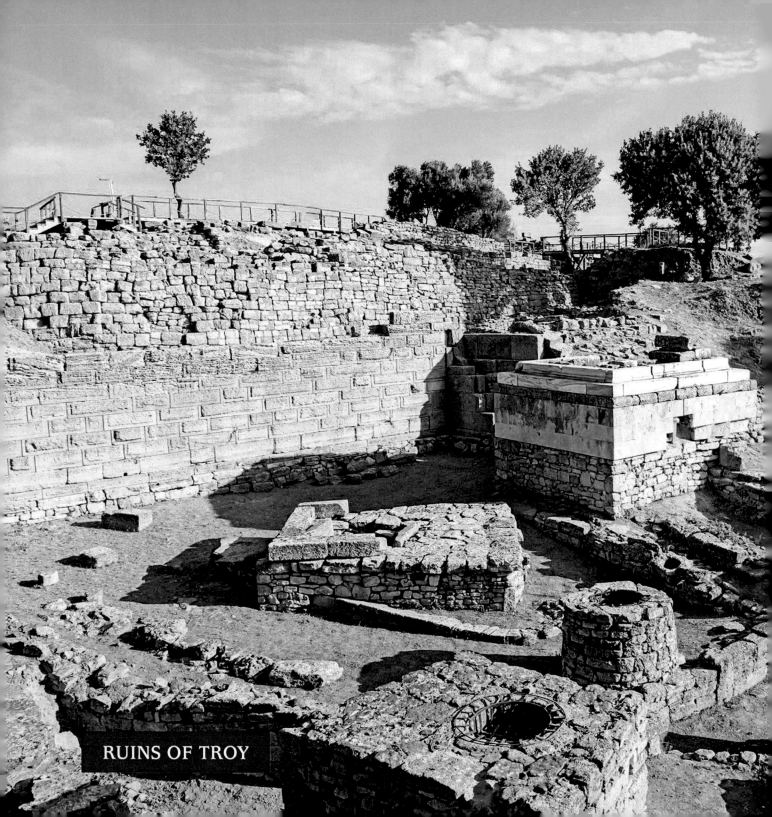

RUINS OF TROY

But Troy was strong and its fighters were fierce. More than once they almost forced the Greeks back to their ships. Odysseus and other leaders would rally the troops by refusing to retreat and calling his men to join with him. He also led nighttime raids against the Trojans.

The Greek army was not always unified. There were jealousies and rivalries. When the great fighter Achilles was killed, both Odysseus and Ajax wanted his armor. Odysseus argued so well that the rest of the Greeks agreed he should get the armor. This made Ajax so furious that he killed himself.

STATUE OF ACHILLES

TO ARTHUR DUKE OF WELLINGTON
AND HIS BRAVE COMPANIONS IN ARMS

THE TROJAN HORSE

Finally, it was Odysseus who planned the trick that defeated the Trojans. The Greeks built a huge wooden horse, hid a group of fighters inside it, and pretended to sail home for Greece with the rest of the army. The Trojans thought the horse was a peace offering and an offering to the gods, and they brought it into their city. At night, the Greek soldiers slipped out of the horse and opened the gates of Troy. The Greek army, which had sailed back during the night, was able to enter the city and conquer Troy.

THE LONG WAY HOME

Now Odysseus and the other Greeks could load up their ships with treasure and sail for home. The trip should have taken just a few weeks, but the gods were angry at Odysseus and they set barrier after barrier between him and his home in Ithaca. Along with winds from the wrong direction for the sailing ships, and the threat of sea monsters, the gods led Odysseus and his men into the path of other threats.

THE LOTUS-EATERS

After escaping a storm sent by the gods, Odysseus and his men land at an island where the inhabitants gave them a narcotic food to eat. The men love the food so much they want to stay on the island, but Odysseus forces them to go on.

On another island, the crew tries to steal sheep for food. The sheep belong to Polyphemus, a cyclops (one-eyed monster) under the protection

of Poseidon, the lord of the sea. Odysseus tricks and blinds Polyphemus, which makes the gods even more angry at him.

ODYSSEUS IN THE CAVE OF THE WINDS

THE BAG OF THE WINDS

Odysseus and his men visit the god of the winds, Aeolus. The god gives Odysseus a bag of mighty wind that he can use if he needs it. But when Ithaca is finally in sight, the men, thinking the bag has treasure in it, open it. This releases the winds which wildly blow the ship across the sea and far away.

CIRCE

On another island the crew meet Circe, who sets them a lovely banquet. Those who eat the food get turned into pigs. Odysseus is barely able to rescue his crew.

CIRCE AND ODYSSEUS

ODYSSEUS

THE UNDERWORLD

Odysseus travels to the underworld and talks with spirits of dead heroes, to gain information he needs for the rest of the trip. Above all, he learns what he should do to make the gods stop being angry with him.

THE SIRENS

Their trip takes them past the island of the Sirens, who sing to draw sailors closer in hopes they will wreck their ships on hidden rocks. Odysseus makes the men fill their ears with wax so they do not hear the song. He has himself tied to the mast so he can hear the singing without being able to respond to it, and is almost driven insane by the desire to go closer to the Sirens.

ODYSSEUS IN FRONT OF SCYLLA AND CHARYBDIS

SCYLLA AND CHARYBDIS

The ships have to pass through a narrow body of water with a monster on one shore and a massive whirlpool near the other shore.

THE CATTLE OF THE SUN

Odysseus and the last members of his crew arrive at an island where Helios, the sun god, keeps wonderful cattle. While Odysseus is away, the men kill and eat some of the cattle. The gods send a storm that destroys the last ship and kills all the crew except Odysseus.

CALYPSO

CALYPSO'S ISLAND

Odysseus, clinging to wreckage from the ship, comes ashore on the island of Calypso, a beautiful nymph with magical powers. She falls in love with him and keeps him a prisoner with her for seven years. Finally, Odysseus gains the pity of some of the gods, who help him escape from Calypso's island. He first lands at Phaeacia, where he tells his story. The people of that place agree to take him the last distance home.

REGAINING ITHACA

By this time Odysseus has been away for twenty years! For all this time Penelope has been loyal to him, sure he will return. But people know that everyone else who survived the Trojan War has made it home long ago. They feel Odysseus must be dead. Over 100 men gather at the king's hall in Ithaca, trying to force Penelope to take one of them to be the new king. Telemachus, Odysseus' son, is afraid to fight so many men at once.

ODYSSEUS

Odysseus returns to Ithaca disguised as a beggar. His dog, whom he last saw when the dog was a puppy, recognizes Odysseus and dies of joy, but nobody else sees through his disguise except Telemachus.

The goddess Athena convinces Penelope to tell the men who would marry her (the Suitors) that whoever can win the competition she will arrange can be her husband. The competition is to string the powerful bow of Odysseus, which he did not take with him to the Trojan War, and fire an arrow through the openings in the heads of twelve axes (the axes were of a design so there was an opening between the back of the axe blade and the handle of the axe).

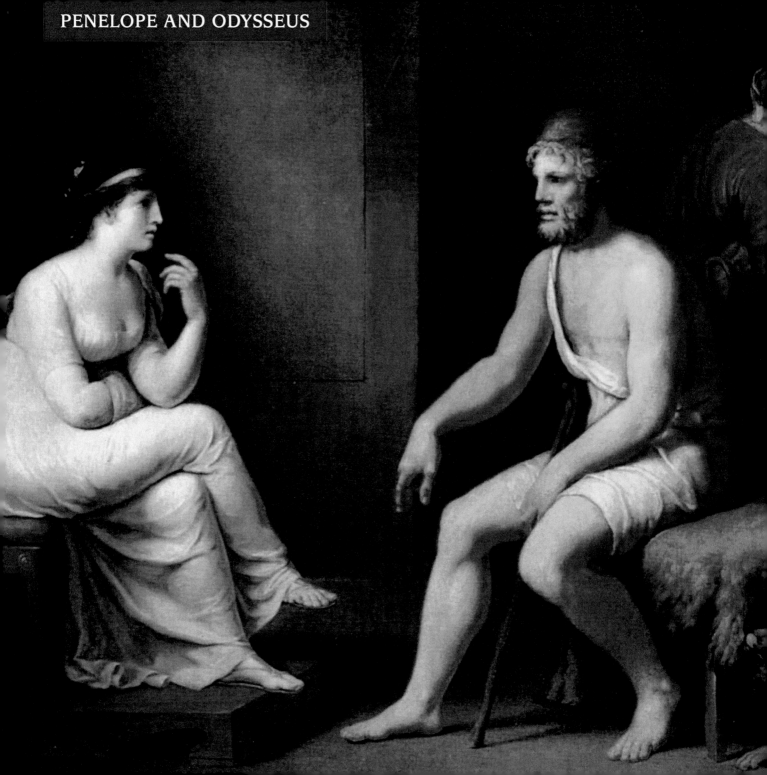

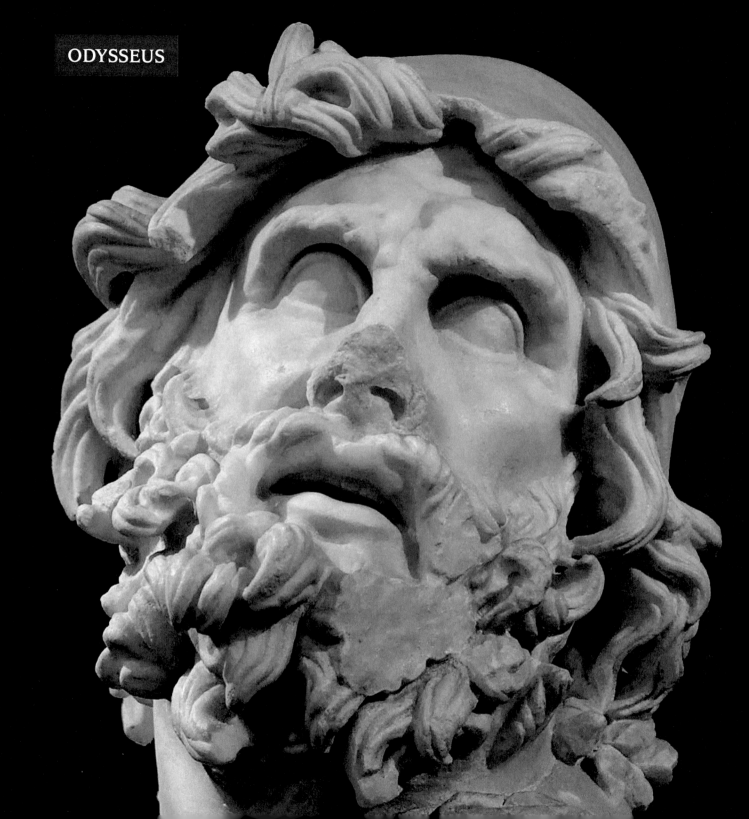

ODYSSEUS

The twelve axes were set up in a row and the suitors began to compete. But none of them could even string the bow. Then Odysseus asks to take a try. He is able to string the bow and shoot the arrow through the axe heads. Then he and Telemachus, with a few loyal men, kill the Suitors.

The families of the dead Suitors come to attack Odysseus in revenge for the loss of their men. They say Odysseus was responsible for the deaths of all those who went with him to Troy, and that now he has killed over one hundred men more.

ODYSSEUS

ATHENA

However, Athena appears and convinces both sides that nothing good would come from more fighting. The island is at peace, and the adventures of Odysseus are at an end as he reunites with Penelope and regains his throne.

LATER LEGENDS

Other writers added Odysseus into their stories, both in classical times and in modern novels and plays. He became a great influence in classical and modern culture, as a man who can fight when he has to but who can solve problems with his wits and with great ability with words whenever possible. He appears in the Aeneid of Virgil, which tells the story of the founding of Rome by refugees from the fall of Troy.

One of the great modern English novels, James Joyce's Ulysses, uses themes from the Odyssey in telling the story of a single day in the life of an Irish man. More recently, Margaret Atwood's The Penelopiad, recounts Odysseus' return to Ithaca from the point of view of his wife, Penelope.

LEARNING FROM THE MYTHS

The great myths and legends are not just idle stories. They helped the people who first heard them understand what it took to be good, noble, and in favor with the gods. What do you find in the myths and legends? Explore further in Baby Professor books like Interesting Facts about Homer's Odyssey.

Made in the USA
San Bernardino, CA
14 March 2019